GW01607218

Two Nonsense Stories

Edward Lear's nonsense poems, such as 'The Owl and the Pussy-Cat' and 'The Jumblies', are perhaps better known than his stories, but only because they are easier to memorize. Although other artists have illustrated later editions of his work, we think that his own scratchy drawings exactly catch the inspired nonsense of his stories.

TWO NONSENSE STORIES

Written and Illustrated by
EDWARD LEAR

A Grasshopper Book
Abelard · London
in association with Richard Sadler

First edition published 1975 by Abelard-Schuman Limited
in association with Richard Sadler
This edition published 1980 by Abelard-Schuman Limited
in association with Richard Sadler

British Library Cataloguing in Publication Data
Lear, Edward
Two nonsense stories. – (Grasshopper books)
I. Title
823'.8 PZ7.L4634

ISBN 0-200-72281-6
ISBN 0-200-72282-4 Pbk

Abelard-Schuman Limited
A Member of The Blackie Group
Furnival House, 14–18 High Holborn
London WC1V 6BX

Printed in Great Britain

THE HISTORY OF THE SEVEN FAMILIES OF THE LAKE PIPPLE–POPPLE.

CHAPTER 1.
INTRODUCTORY.

In former days—that is to say, once upon a time, there lived in the Land of Gramblamble, Seven Families. They lived by the side of the great Lake Pipple-Popple (one of the Seven Families, indeed, lived *in* the Lake), and on the outskirts of the City of Tosh, which, excepting when it was quite dark, they could see plainly. The names of all these places you have probably heard of, and you have only not to look in your

Geography books to find out all about them.

Now the Seven Families who lived on the borders of the great Lake Pipple-Popple, were as follows in the next Chapter.

CHAPTER II
THE SEVEN FAMILIES.

There was a family of Two old Parrots and Seven young Parrots.

There was a family of Two old Storks and Seven young Storks.

There was a family of Two old Geese and Seven young Geese.

There was a family of Two old Owls and Seven young Owls.

There was a family of Two old Guinea Pigs and Seven young Guinea Pigs.

There was a Family of Two old Cats and Seven young Cats.

And there was a family of Two old Fishes and Seven young Fishes.

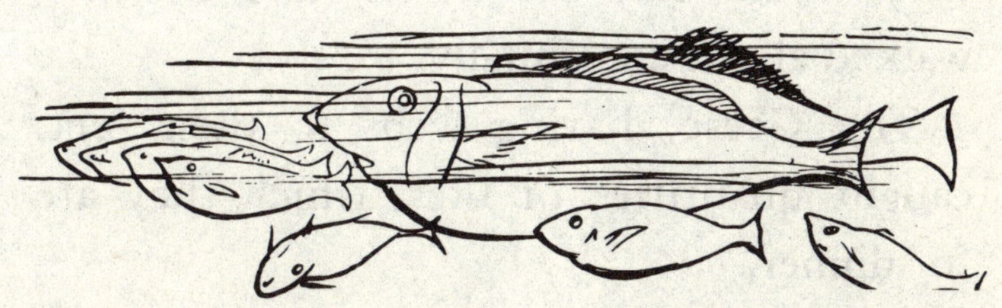

CHAPTER III.

THE HABITS OF THE SEVEN FAMILIES.

The Parrots lived upon the Soffsky-Poffsky trees,– which were beautiful to behold, and covered with blue leaves,–and they fed upon fruit, artichokes, and striped beetles.

The Storks walked in and out of the Lake Pipple-Popple and ate frogs for breakfast and buttered toast for tea; but on account of the extreme length of their legs, they could not sit down, and so they walked about continually.

The Geese, having webs to their feet, caught quantities of flies, which they ate for dinner.

The Owls anxiously looked after mice, which they caught and made into sago puddings.

The Guinea Pigs toddled about the gardens, and ate lettuces and Cheshire cheese.

The Cats sat still in the sunshine, and fed upon sponge biscuits.

The Fishes lived in the Lake, and fed chiefly on boiled periwinkles.

And all these Seven Families lived together in the utmost fun and felicity.

CHAPTER IV
THE CHILDREN OF THE SEVEN FAMILIES ARE SENT AWAY.

One day all the Seven Fathers and the Seven Mothers of the Seven Families agreed that they would send their children out to see the world.

So they called them all together, and gave them each eight shillings and some good advice, some chocolate drops, and a small green morocco pocket-book to set down their expenses in.

They then particularly entreated them not to quarrel, and all the parents sent off their children with a parting injunction.

"If," said the old Parrots, "you find a Cherry, do not fight about who shall have it."

"And," said the old Storks, "if you find a Frog, divide it carefully into seven bits, but on no account quarrel about it."

And the old Geese said to the Seven young Geese, "Whatever you do, be sure you do not touch a Plum-pudding Flea."

And the old Owls said, "If you find a Mouse, tear him up into seven slices, and eat him cheerfully, but without quarrelling."

And the old Guinea Pigs said, "Have a care that you eat your Lettuces, should you find any, not greedily but calmly."

And the old Cats said, "Be particularly careful not to meddle with a Clangle-Wangle, if you should see one."

And the old Fishes said, "Above all

things avoid eating a blue Boss-Woss, for they do not agree with Fishes, and give them a pain in their toes."

So all the Children of each Family thanked their parents, and making in all forty-nine polite bows, they went into the wide world.

CHAPTER V.
THE HISTORY OF THE SEVEN YOUNG PARROTS.

The Seven young Parrots had not gone far, when they saw a tree with a single Cherry on it, which the oldest Parrot picked instantly, but the other six being extremely hungry, tried to get it also. On which all the Seven began to fight, and they scuffled,

and huffled,
and ruffled,
and shuffled,
and puffled,
and muffled,

and buffled,

and duffled,

and fluffled,

and guffled,

and bruffled, and screamed, and shrieked, and squealed, and squeaked, and clawed, and snapped, and bit, and bumped, and thumped, and dumped, and flumped each other, till they were all torn into little bits, and at last there was nothing left to record this painful incident, except the Cherry and seven small green feathers.

And that was the vicious and voluble end of the Seven young Parrots.

CHAPTER VI.
THE HISTORY OF THE SEVEN YOUNG STORKS.

When the Seven young Storks set out, they walked or flew for fourteen weeks in a straight line, and for six weeks more in a crooked one; and after that they ran as hard as they could for one hundred and eight miles; and after that they stood still and made a himmeltanious chatter-clatter-blattery noise with their bills.

About the same time they perceived a large Frog, spotted with green, and with a sky-blue stripe under each ear.

So being hungry, they immediately flew

at him and were going to divide him into seven pieces, when they began to quarrel as to which of his legs should be taken off first. One said this, and another said that, and while they were all quarrelling the Frog hopped away. And when they saw that he was gone, they began to chatter-clatter,

blatter-platter,

patter-blatter,

matter-clatter,

flatter-quatter, more violently

than ever. And after they had fought for a week they pecked each other to little pieces, so that at last nothing was left of any of them except their bills.

And that was the end of the Seven young Storks.

CHAPTER VII.
THE HISTORY OF THE SEVEN YOUNG GEESE.

When the Seven young Geese began to travel, they went over a large plain, on which there was but one tree, and that was a very bad one.

So four of them went up to the top of it, and looked about them, while the other three waddled up and down, and repeated poetry, and their last six lessons in Arithmetic, Geography, and Cookery.

Presently they perceived, a long way off, an object of the most interesting and obese appearance, having a perfectly round body, exactly resembling a boiled plum-pudding, with two little wings, and a beak, and three feathers growing out of his head, and only one leg.

So after a time all the Seven young Geese said to each other, "Beyond all doubt this beast must be a Plum-pudding Flea!"

On which they incautiously began to sing aloud,

"Plum-pudding Flea,
"Plum-pudding Flea,
"Wherever you be,
"O come to our tree,
"And listen, O listen, O listen to me!"

And no sooner had they sung this verse than the Plum-pudding Flea began to hop and skip on his one leg with the most dreadful velocity, and came straight to the tree, where he stopped and looked about him in a vacant and voluminous manner.

On which the Seven young Geese were greatly alarmed, and all of a tremble-bemble; so one of them put out his long neck and just touched him with the tip of his bill,—but no sooner had he done this than the Plum-pudding Flea skipped and hopped about more and more and higher and higher, after which he opened his mouth, and to the great surprise and indignation of the Seven Geese, began to bark so loudly and furiously and terribly that they were totally unable to bear the noise, and by degrees every one of them suddenly tumbled down quite dead.

So that was the end of the Seven young Geese.

CHAPTER VIII.
THE HISTORY OF THE SEVEN YOUNG OWLS.

When the Seven young Owls set out, they sat every now and then on the branches of old trees, and never went far at one time.

And one night when it was quite dark, they thought they heard a mouse, but as the gas lamps were not lighted, they could not see him.

So they called out, "Is that a mouse?"

On which a Mouse answered, "Squeaky-peeky-weeky, yes it is."

And immediately all the young Owls

threw themselves off the tree, meaning to alight on the ground; but they did not perceive that there was a large well below them, into which they all fell superficially, and were every one of them drowned in less than half a minute.

So that was the end of the Seven young Owls.

CHAPTER IX.
THE HISTORY OF THE SEVEN YOUNG GUINEA PIGS.

The Seven young Guinea Pigs went into a garden full of Gooseberry-bushes and Tiggory-trees, under one of which they fell asleep. When they awoke they saw a large Lettuce which had grown out of the ground while they had been sleeping, and which had an immense number of green leaves. At which they all exclaimed,

"Lettuce! O Lettuce!
"Let us, O let us,
"O Lettuce leaves,

"O let us leave this tree and eat
"Lettuce, O let us, Lettuce leaves!"

And instantly the Seven young Guinea Pigs rushed with such extreme force against the Lettuce-plant, and hit their heads so vividly against its stalk, that the concussion brought on directly an incipient transitional inflammation of their noses, which grew worse and worse and worse till it incidentally killed them all Seven.

And that was the end of the Seven young Guinea Pigs.

CHAPTER X.

THE HISTORY OF THE SEVEN YOUNG CATS.

The Seven young Cats set off on their travels with great delight and rapacity. But, on coming to the top of a high hill, they perceived at a long distance of a Clangle-Wangle (or, as it is more properly written, Clangel-Wangel), and in spite of the warning they had had, they ran straight up to it.

(Now the Clangle-Wangle is a most dangerous and delusive beast, and by no means commonly to be met with. They live in the water as well as on land, using their long tail as a sail when in the former element. Their speed is extreme, but their habits of life are domestic and superfluous, and their general demeanour pensive and pellucid. On summer evenings they may sometimes be observed near the Lake Pipple-popple, standing on their heads and humming their national melodies: they subsist entirely on vegetables, excepting when they eat veal, or mutton, or pork, or beef, or fish, or saltpetre.)

The moment the Clangle-Wangle saw the Seven young Cats approach, he ran away; and as he ran straight on four four months, and the Cats, though they continued to run, could never overtake him,—they all gradually *died* of fatigue and exhaustion, and never afterwards recovered.

And this was the end of the Seven young Cats.

CHAPTER XI.
THE HISTORY OF THE SEVEN FISHES.

The Seven young Fishes swam across the Lake Pipple-popple, and into the river, and into the ocean, where most unhappily for them they saw, on the fifteenth day of their travels, a bright-blue Boss-Woss, and instantly swam after him. But the Blue Boss-Woss plunged into a perpendicular,

spicular,

orbicular,

quadrangular,

circular depth of soft mud,

where in fact his house was.

And the Seven young Fishes, swimming with great and uncomfortable velocity, plunged also into the mud, quite against their will, and not being accustomed to it, were all suffocated in a very short period.

And that was the end of the Seven young Fishes.

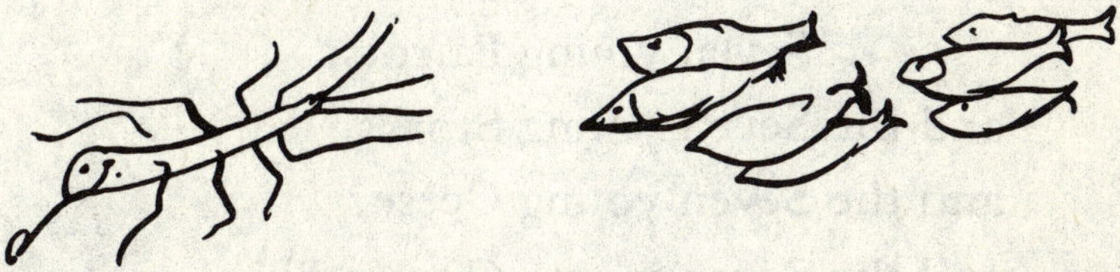

CHAPTER XII.
OF WHAT OCCURRED SUBSEQUENTLY

After it was known that the
Seven young Parrots,
and the Seven young Storks,
and the Seven young Geese,
and the Seven young Guinea Pigs,
and the Seven young Cats,
and the Seven young Fishes,
were all dead, then the Frog, and the Plum-pudding Flea, and the Mouse, and the Clangel-Wangel, and the Blue Boss-Woss, all met together to rejoice over their good fortune. And they collected the Seven

Feathers of the Seven young Parrots, and the Seven Bills of the Seven young Storks, and the Lettuce, and the Cherry, and having placed the latter on the Lettuce, and the other objects in a circular arrangement at their base, they danced a hornpipe round all these memorials until they were quite tired; after which they gave a tea-party, and a garden-party, and a ball, and a concert, and then returned to their respective homes full of joy and respect, sympathy, satisfaction, and disgust.

CHAPTER XIII.
OF WHAT BECAME OF THE PARENTS OF THE FORTY–NINE CHILDREN.

But when the two old Parrots,
and the two old Storks,
and the two old Geese,
and the two old Owls,
and the two old Guinea Pigs,
and the two old Cats,
and the two old Fishes,

became aware, by reading in the newspapers, of the calamitous extinction of the whole of their families, they refused all further sustenance; and sending out to various shops, they purchased great quantities of Cayenne Pepper, and Brandy, and Vinegar, and blue Sealing-wax, besides Seven immense glass Bottles with air-tight stoppers. And having done this, they ate a light supper of brown bread and Jerusalem Artichokes, and took an affecting and formal leave of the whole of their acquaintance, which was very numerous and distinguished, and select, and responsible, and ridiculous.

CHAPTER XIV.
CONCLUSION.

And after this, they filled the bottles with the ingredients for pickling, and each couple jumped into a separate bottle, by which effort of course they all died immediately, and became thoroughly pickled in a few minutes; having previously made their wills (by the assistance of the most eminent Lawyers of the District), in which they left strict orders that the Stoppers of the Seven Bottles should be carefully sealed up with the blue Sealing-wax they had purchased; and that they themselves in the Bottles should be presented to the principal museum of the city of Tosh, to be labelled with Parchment or any other anti-congenial succedaneum, and to be placed on a marble table with silver-gilt legs, for the daily inspection and contemplation, and for the perpetual benefit of the pusillanimous public.

And if ever you happen to go to Gramble-Blamble, and visit that museum in the city of Tosh, look for them on the Ninety-eighth table in the Four hundred and twenty-seventh room of the right-hand corridor of the left wing of the Central Quadrangle of that magnificent building; for if you do not, you certainly will not see them.

THE STORY OF THE FOUR LITTLE CHILDREN WHO WENT ROUND THE WORLD.

Once upon a time, a long while ago, there were four little people whose names were Violet, Slingsby, Guy, and Lionel;

VIOLET, SLINGSBY, GUY, and LIONEL;

and they all thought they should like to see the world. So they bought a large boat to sail quite round the world by sea, and then they were to come back on the other side by land. The boat was painted blue with green spots, and the sail was yellow with red stripes; and when they set off, they only took a small Cat to steer and look after the boat, besides an elderly Quangle-Wangle, who had to cook the dinner and make the tea; for which purposes they took a large kettle.

For the first ten days they sailed on beautifully, and found plenty to eat, as there were lots of fish, and they had only to take them out of the sea with a long spoon, when the Quangle-Wangle instantly cooked them, and the Pussy-Cat was fed with the bones, with which she expressed herself pleased on the whole, so that all the party were very happy.

During the day-time, Violet chiefly occupied herself in putting salt-water into a churn, while her three brothers churned it violently, in the hope that it would turn into butter, which it seldom, if ever did;

and in the evening they all retired into the Tea-kettle, where they all managed to sleep very comfortably, while Pussy and the Quangle-Wangle managed the boat.

After a time they saw some land at a distance; and when they came to it, they found it was an island made of water quite surrounded by earth. Besides that, it was bordered by evanescent isthmuses with a great Gulf-stream running about all over it, so that it was perfectly beautiful, and contained only a single tree, 503 feet high.

When they had landed, they walked about, but found to their great surprise that the island was quite full of veal-cutlets and chocolate-drops, and nothing else. So they all climbed up the single high tree to discover, if possible, if there were any people; but having remained on the top of the tree for a week, and not seeing any body, they naturally concluded that there were no inhabitants, and accordingly when they came down they loaded the boat with two thousand veal-cutlets and a million of chocolate drops, and these afforded them sustenance for more than a month, during which time they pursued their voyage with the utmost delight and apathy.

After this they came to a shore where there were no less than sixty-five great red parrots with blue tails, sitting on a rail all of a row, and all fast asleep. And I am sorry to say that the Pussy-Cat and the Quangle-Wangle crept softly and bit off the tail-

feathers of all the sixty-five parrots, for which Violet reproved them both severely.

Notwithstanding which, she proceeded to insert all the feathers, two hundred and

sixty in number, in her bonnet, thereby causing it to have a lovely and glittering appearance, highly prepossessing and efficacious.

The next thing that happened to them was in a narrow part of the sea, which was so entirely full of fishes that the boat could go on no further; so they remained there about six weeks, till they had eaten nearly all the fishes, which were Soles, and all ready-cooked and covered with shrimp

sauce, so that there was no trouble whatever. And as the few fishes who remained uneaten complained of the cold, as well as of the difficulty they had in getting any sleep on account of the extreme noise made by the Arctic Bears and the Tropical Turnspits, which frequented the neighbourhood in great numbers, Violet most amiably knitted a small woollen frock for several of the fishes, and Slingsby administered some opium drops to them, through which kindess they became quite warm and slept soundly.

Then they came to a country which was wholly covered with immense Orange-trees of a vast size, and quite full of fruit. So they all landed, taking with them the Tea-kettle, intending to gather some of the Oranges and place them in it. But while they were busy about this, a most dreadfully high wind rose, and blew out most of the parrot-tail feathers from Violet's bonnet. That, however, was nothing compared with the calamity of the Oranges falling down on their heads by millions and millions, which thumped and bumped and bumped and thumped them all so seriously that they were obliged to run as hard as they could for their lives, besides that the sound of the Oranges rattling on the Tea-kettle was of the most fearful and amazing nature.

Nevertheless they got safely to the boat, although considerably vexed and hurt; and the Quangle-Wangle's right foot was so

knocked about that he had to sit with his head in his slipper for at least a week.

This event made them all for a time rather melancholy, and perhaps they might never have become less so, had not Lionel, with a most praiseworthy devotion and perseverance, continued to stand on one leg

and whistle to them in a loud and lively manner, which diverted the whole party so extremely, that they gradually recovered their spirits, and agreed that whenever they should reach home they would subscribe towards a testimony to Lionel, entirely made of Gingerbread and Raspberries, as an earnest token of their sincere and grateful infection.

After sailing on calmly for several more days, they came to another country, where they were much pleased and surprised to see a countless multitude of white Mice with red eyes, all sitting in a great circle, slowly eating Custard Pudding with the most satisfactory and polite demeanour.

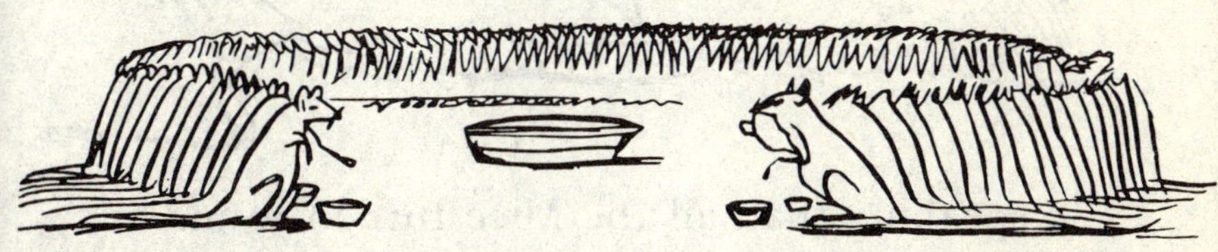

And as the four Travellers were rather hungry, being tired of eating nothing but Soles and Oranges for so long a period, they held a council as to the propriety of asking the Mice for some of their pudding in a humble and affecting manner, by which they could hardly be otherwise than gratified. It was agreed therefore that Guy should go and ask the Mice, which he immediately did; and the result was that they gave a Walnut-shell only half full of Custard diluted with water. Now, this displeased Guy, who said, "Out of such a lot of Pudding as you have got, I must say you might have spared a somewhat larger quantity!" But no sooner had he finished

speaking than all the Mice turned round at once, and sneezed at him in an appalling and vindictive manner, (and it is impossible to imagine a more scroobious and unpleasant sound than that caused by the simultaneous sneezing of many millions of angry Mice,) so that Guy rushed back to the boat, having first shied his cap into the middle of the Custard Pudding, by which means he completely spoiled the Mice's dinner.

By-and-by the Four Children came to a

country where there were no houses, but only an incredibly innumerable number of large bottles without corks, and of a dazzling and sweetly susceptible blue colour. Each of these blue bottles contained a Blue-Bottle-Fly, and all these interesting animals live continually together in the most copious and rural harmony, nor perhaps in many parts of the world is such perfect and abject happiness to be found. Violet, and Slingsby, and Guy, and Lionel, were greatly struck with this singular and instructive settlement, and having previously asked permission of the Blue-Bottle-Flies, (which was most courteously granted,) the boat was drawn up to the shore, and they proceeded to make tea in front of the bottles; but as they had no tea-leaves, they merely placed some pebbles in the hot water, and the Quangle-Wangle played some tunes over it on an Accordion, by which of course tea was made directly, and of the very best quality.

The Four Children then entered into conversation with the Blue-Bottle-Flies, who discoursed in a placid and genteel manner, though with a slightly buzzing accent, chiefly owing to the fact that they each held a small clothes-brush between their teeth, which naturally occasioned a fizzy extraneous utterance.

"Why," said Violet, "would you kindly inform us, do you reside in bottles? and if in bottles at all, why not rather in green or purple, or indeed in yellow bottles?"

To which questions a very aged Blue-Bottle-Fly answered, "We found the bottles here all ready to live in, that is to say, our great-great-great-great-great-grandfathers did, so we occupied them at once. And when the winter comes on, we turn the bottles upside-down, and consequently rarely feel the cold at all, and you know very well that this could not be the case with bottles of any other colour than blue."

"Of course it could not," said Slingsby; "but if we may take the liberty of inquiring, on what do you chiefly subsist?"

"Mainly on Oyster-patties," said the Blue-Bottle-Fly, "and when these are scarce, on Raspberry Vinegar and Russian leather boiled down to a jelly."

"How delicious!" said Guy.

To which Lionel added, "Huzz!" and all the Blue-Bottle-Flies said "Buzz!"

At this time, an elderly Fly said it was the hour for the Evening-song to be sung; and on a signal being given all the Blue-Bottle-Flies began to buzz at once in a sumptuous and sonorous manner, the melodious and mucilaginous sounds echoing all over the waters, and resounding across the tumultuous tops of the transitory Titmice upon the intervening and verdant mountains, with a serene and sickly suavity only known to the truly virtuous. The Moon was shining slobaciously from the star-bespangled sky, while her light irrigated the smooth and shiny sides and wings and backs of the Blue-Bottle-Flies with a peculiar and trivial splendour, while all nature cheerfully responded to the cirulaean and conspicuous circumstances.

In many long-after years, the four little Travellers looked back to that evening as one of the happiest in all their lives, and it was already past midnight, when—the sail of the boat having been set up by the Quangle-Wangle, the Tea-kettle and Churn placed in their respective positions, and the Pussy-Cat stationed at the helm—the Children each took a last and affectionate farewell of the Blue-Bottle-Flies, who walked down in a body to the water's edge to see the Travellers embark.

As a token of parting respect and esteem, Violet made a curtsey quite down to the ground, and stuck one of her few

remaining Parrot-tail feathers into the back hair of the most pleasing of the Blue-Bottle-Flies, while Slingsby, Guy, and Lionel offered them three small boxes, containing respectively Black Pins, Dried Figs, and Epsom Salts: and thus they left that happy shore for ever.

Overcome by their feelings, the four little Travellers instantly jumped into the Tea-kettle, and fell fast asleep. But all along the shore for many hours there was distincly heard a sound of severely suppressed sobs, and a vague multitude of living creatures using their pocket-handkerchiefs in a subdued simultaneous snuffle—lingering sadly along the wallopping waves, as the boat sailed farther and farther away from the Land of the Happy Blue-Bottle-Flies.

Nothing particular occurred for some days after these events, except that as the Travellers were passing a low tract of sand, they perceived an unusual and gratifying spectacle, namely, a large number of Crabs and Crawfish—perhaps six or seven hundred—sitting by the waterside, and endeavouring to disentangle a vast heap of pale pink worsted, which they moistened at intervals with a fluid composed of Lavender-water and White-wine Negus.

"Can we be of any service to you, O crusty Crabbies?" said the Four Children.

"Thank you kindly," said the Crabs,

consecutively. "We are trying to make some worsted Mittens, but do not know how."

On which Violet, who was perfectly acquainted with the art of mitten-making, said to the Crabs, "Do your claws unscrew, or are they fixtures?"

"They are all made to unscrew," said the Crabs, and forthwith they deposited a great pile of claws close to the boat, with which Violet uncombed all the pale pink worsted, and then made the loveliest Mittens with it you can imagine. These the Crabs, having resumed and screwed on their claws, placed cheerfully upon their wrists, and walked away rapidly, on their hind legs, warbling songs with a silvery voice and in a minor key.

After this the four little people sailed on again till they came to a vast and wide plain of astonishing dimensions, on which nothing whatever could be discovered at first; but as the Travellers walked onward, there appeared in the extreme and dim distance a single object, which on a nearer approach, and on an accurately cutaneous inspection, seemed to be somebody in a large white wig sitting on an arm-chair made of Sponge Cakes and Oyster-shells. "It does not quite look like a human being," said Violet doubtfully; nor could they make out what it really was, till the Quangle-Wangle (who had previously been round the world) exclaimed softly in a loud voice, "It is the Co-operative Cauliflower!"

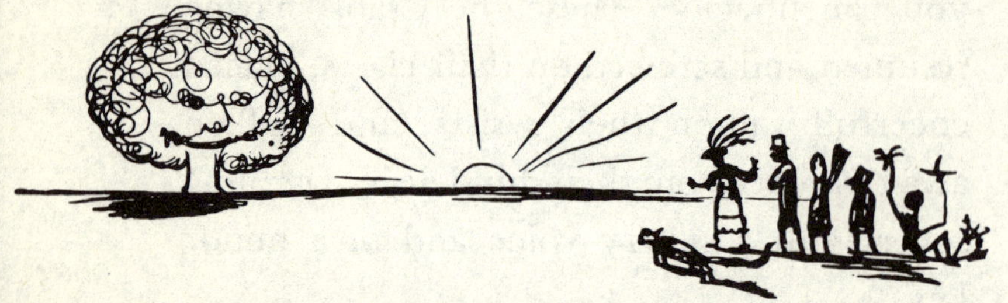

And so in truth it was, and they soon found that what they had taken for an immense wig was in reality the top of the cauliflower, and that he had no feet at all, being able to walk tolerably well with a fluctuating and graceful movement on a single cabbage stalk, an accomplishment which naturally saved him the expense of stockings and shoes.

Presently, while the whole party from the boat was gazing at him with mingled affection and disgust, he suddenly arose, and in a somewhat plumdomphious manner hurried off towards the setting sun,—his steps supported by two superincumbent

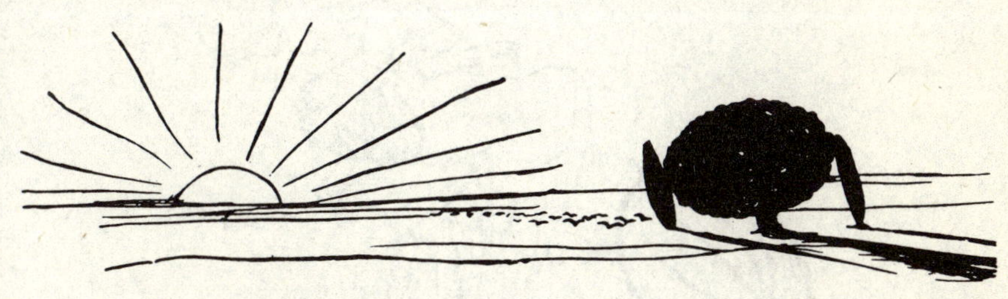

confidential cucumbers, and a large number of Waterwagtails proceeding in advance of him by three-and-three in a row,—till he finally disappeared on the brink of the western sky in a crystal cloud of sudorific sand.

So remarkable a sight of course impressed the Four Children very deeply; and they returned immediately to their boat with a strong sense of undeveloped asthma and a great appetite.

Shortly after this the Travellers were obliged to sail directly below some high

overhanging rocks, from the top of one of which a particularly odious little boy, dressed in rose-coloured knickerbockers, and with a pewter plate upon his head, threw an enormous Pumpkin at the boat, by which it was instantly upset.

But this upsetting was of no consequence, because all the party knew how to swim very well, and in fact they preferred swimming about till after the moon rose, when, the water growing chilly, they sponge-taneously entered the boat. Meanwhile the Quangle-Wangle threw back the Pumpkin with immense force, so that it hit the rocks where the malicious little boy in rose-coloured knickerbockers was sitting, when, being quite full of Lucifer-matches, the Pumpkin exploded surreptitiously into a thousand bits, whereon the rocks instantly took fire, and the odious little boy became unpleasantly hotter and hotter and hotter, till his knickerbockers were turned quite green, and his nose was burned off.

Two or three days after this had happened they came to another place, where they found nothing at all except some wide and deep pits full of Mulberry Jam. This is the property of the tiny yellow-nosed Apes who abound in these districts, and who store up the Mulberry Jam for their food in winter, when they mix it with pellucid pale perwinkle soup, and serve it out in Wedgwood China bowls, which grow freely all over that part of the country. Only one of the Yellow-nosed Apes was on the spot, and he was fast asleep; yet the Four Travellers and the Quangle-Wangle and Pussy were so terrified by the violence and sanguinary sound of his snoring, that they merely took a small cupful of the Jam, and returned to re-embark in their boat without delay.

What was their horror on seeing the boat (including the Churn and the Tea-kettle) in the mouth of an enormous Seeze Pyder, an aquatic and ferocious creature truly dreadful to behold, and happily only met with in those excessive longitudes. In a moment

the beautiful boat was bitten into fifty-five-thousand-million-hundred-billion bits; and it instantly became quite clear that Violet, Slingsby, Guy, and Lionel could no longer preliminate their voyage by sea.

The Four Travellers were therefore obliged to resolve on pursuing their wanderings by land, and very fortunately there happened to pass by at that moment an elderly Rhinoceros, on which they seized; and all four mounting on his back, the Quangle-Wangle sitting on his horn and holding on by his ears, and the Pussy-Cat swinging at the end of his tail, they set off, having only four small beans and three pounds of mashed potatoes to last through their whole journey.

They were, however, able to catch numbers of the chickens and turkeys and other birds who incessantly alighted on the head of the Rhinoceros for the purpose of gathering the seeds of the rhododendron plants which grew there, and these

creatures they cooked in the most translucent and satisfactory manner, by means of a fire lighted on the end of the Rhinoceros back. A crowd of Kangaroos and

Gigantic Cranes accompanied them, from feelings of curiosity and complacency, so that they were never at a loss for company, and went onward as it were in a sort of profuse and triumphant procession.

Thus, in less than eighteen weeks, they all arrived safely at home, where they were received by their admiring relatives with joy tempered with contempt; and where they finally resolved to carry out the rest of their travelling plans at some more favourable opportunity.

As for the Rhinoceros, in token of their grateful adherence, they had him killed and stuffed directly, and then set him up outside the door of their father's house as a Diaphanous Doorscraper.